The KidHaven Health Library

What Happens When Someone Has
ASTHMA?

By Katie Kawa

KidHaven
PUBLISHING

Published in 2020 by
KidHaven Publishing, an Imprint of Greenhaven Publishing, LLC
353 3rd Avenue
Suite 255
New York, NY 10010

Designer: Andrea Davison-Bartolotta
Editor: Katie Kawa

Photo credits: Cover Vitaliy Karimov/Shutterstock.com; p. 5 (main) Lopolo/Shutterstock.com; p. 5 (inset) KadirKARA/Shutterstock.com; p. 6 Natee K Jindakum/Shutterstock.com; p. 7 BlueRingMedia/ Shutterstock.com; p. 8 Antonio Guillem/Shutterstock.com; pp. 9, 13 Pixel-Shot/Shutterstock.com; p. 10 mimagephotography/Shutterstock.com; p. 12 Microgen/Shutterstock.com; p. 14 Fabio Diena/Shutterstock.com; pp. 15, 18 Monkey Business Images/Shutterstock.com; p. 16 JohnKwan/ Shutterstock.com; pp. 17, 22, 23 BSIP/UIG Via Getty Images; p. 19 IAN HOOTON/SPL/Getty Images; p. 20 Brian Chase/Shutterstock.com; p. 21 michaeljung/Shutterstock.com; p. 25 Alexander_Safonov/ Shutterstock.com; p. 26 VGstockstudio/Shutterstock.com; p. 29 Zulfiya887/Shutterstock.com.

Library of Congress Cataloging-in-Publication Data

Names: Kawa, Katie, author.
Title: What happens when someone has asthma? / Katie Kawa.
Description: First edition. | New York : KidHaven Publishing, [2020] |
    Series: The KidHaven health library | Includes bibliographical
    references and index. | Audience: Ages 9 | Audience: Grades 4-6
Identifiers: LCCN 2019031206 (print) | LCCN 2019031207 (ebook) | ISBN
    9781534532472 (library binding) | ISBN 9781534532601 (paperback) | ISBN
    9781534532663 (set) | ISBN 9781534532519 (ebook)
Subjects: LCSH: Asthma in children–Juvenile literature. | Asthma–Juvenile
    literature.
Classification: LCC RJ436.A8 K39 2020 (print) | LCC RJ436.A8 (ebook) |
    DDC 618.92/238–dc23
LC record available at https://lccn.loc.gov/2019031206
LC ebook record available at https://lccn.loc.gov/2019031207

Printed in the United States of America

Some of the images in this book illustrate individuals who are models. The depictions do not imply actual situations or events.

CPSIA compliance information: Batch #BW20KL: For further information contact Greenhaven Publishing LLC, New York, New York at 1-844-317-7404.

Please visit our website, www.greenhavenpublishing.com. For a free color catalog of all our high-quality books, call toll free 1-844-317-7404 or fax 1-844-317-7405.

Contents

BREATHING EASIER

When something is simple, people often say it's "as easy as breathing." However, for some people, breathing isn't easy! When someone has a health problem known as asthma, the airways that let air in and out of their lungs swell and get smaller. This causes them to cough, makes their chest feel tight, and can make it very hard for them to breathe.

Asthma affects millions of people around the world, and it's a problem many kids deal with every day. Doctors call it a chronic health problem, which means it doesn't go away, and there's currently no cure for asthma.

Although asthma can be a serious problem, there are many **treatments** available for people with this condition. Thanks to these treatments, people with asthma can breathe easier!

Asthma by the Numbers

The World Health Organization, which tracks the health of people around the world, has stated that more than 230 million people on Earth have asthma. In the United States alone, more than 25 million people are living with this condition, and more than 6 million of those Americans are kids. Asthma is more common in children than it is in adults, but some adults can first show signs of asthma later in life.

World Health Organization logo

Many people with asthma use a tool called an inhaler to take medicine that helps them feel better. How does an inhaler work? Keep reading to find out!

ASTHMA AND THE AIRWAYS

Asthma is a health problem that affects a person's respiratory system, which is the body system that controls breathing. Air goes in and out of the lungs through airways that are also called bronchial tubes. When a person has asthma, their airways become inflamed, or swollen. This makes the tubes smaller, which means less air can get in and out of the lungs.

Common symptoms, or signs, of asthma include a cough that won't go away and shortness of breath. Another symptom people often deal with is wheezing, which is a whistling sound that comes from the chest when someone with asthma tries to breathe.

Different for Everyone

Asthma doesn't affect everyone who has it the same way. For example, some people might not deal with asthma symptoms often, while others have a constant cough. The things that make a person's asthma get worse—known as triggers—also differ from person to person. While one person with asthma might have a hard time exercising, another might have trouble breathing after sitting outside. Only a doctor can tell for sure if a person has asthma.

If you have any of these symptoms, talk to a trusted adult about them. They can take you to the doctor, and you can start feeling better soon.

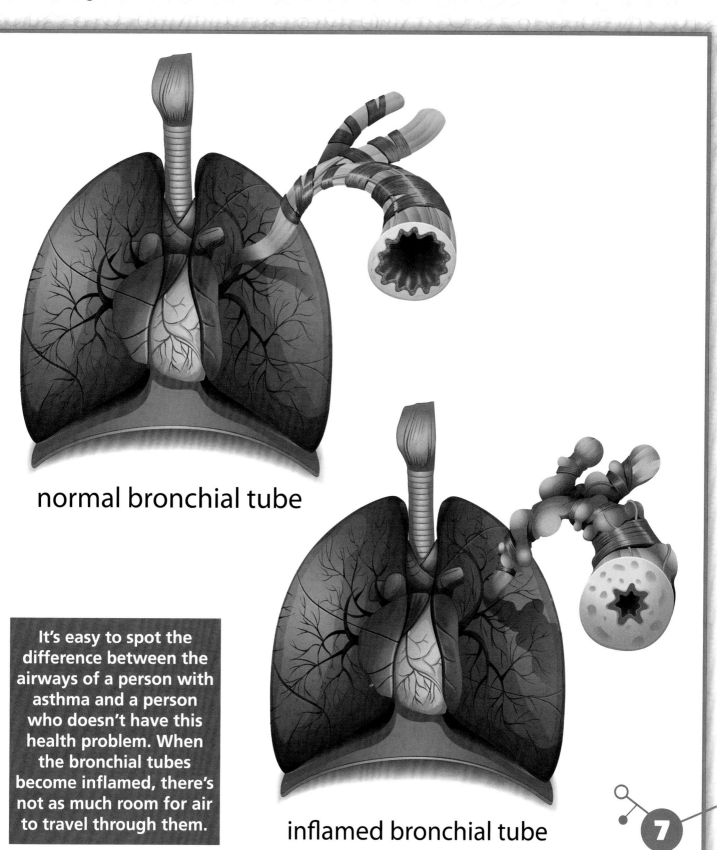

normal bronchial tube

It's easy to spot the difference between the airways of a person with asthma and a person who doesn't have this health problem. When the bronchial tubes become inflamed, there's not as much room for air to travel through them.

inflamed bronchial tube

ASTHMA ATTACKS

Sometimes, a person's asthma symptoms get worse very quickly. This is called an asthma attack. An asthma attack is caused by a person breathing in an asthma trigger, such as smoke, dust, or cold air. It can also be caused by an illness such as the flu.

How to Help

If you see someone having an asthma attack, it can be very scary, but there are some things you can do to help them. The most important thing is to stay calm. If you can, ask an adult nearby for help. If there's no adult nearby, get the person having the attack away from any triggers, make sure they're sitting up, and ask them if they have an asthma action plan you can help them follow. Also, if they have an inhaler, help them get it, and make sure they use it.

During an asthma attack, a person's airways become even more inflamed, and the muscles around them get very tight. Their body also produces more or thicker mucus. This is a **fluid** the body makes to get rid of dust and other things in the nose and lungs that aren't supposed to be there.

In some cases, an asthma attack can be deadly. Getting help quickly during an asthma attack can save someone's life!

An asthma attack is sometimes called an asthma flare-up or episode. No matter what you call it, it's a serious problem that needs to be treated right away.

KNOW YOUR TRIGGERS!

How can someone with asthma avoid having an asthma attack? One of the most important ways to prevent an asthma attack is to identify asthma triggers. When someone with asthma is exposed to a trigger, it can make their symptoms worse and cause an asthma attack.

Common asthma triggers include pollen and certain chemicals. Air pollution has also been known to cause asthma symptoms to get worse. Smoke is another asthma trigger, so it's

Asthma and Emotions

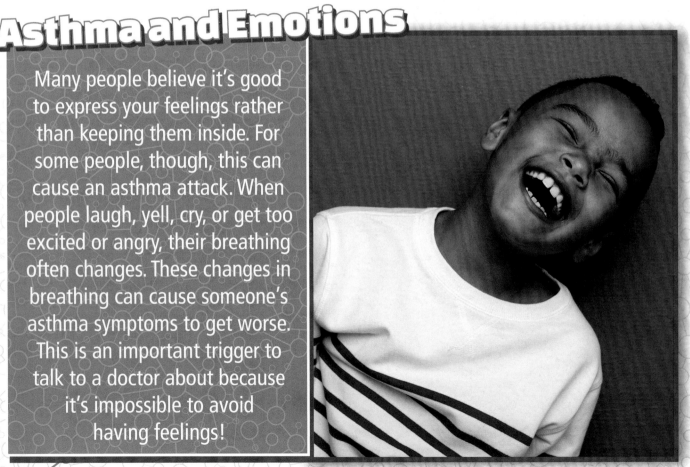

Many people believe it's good to express your feelings rather than keeping them inside. For some people, though, this can cause an asthma attack. When people laugh, yell, cry, or get too excited or angry, their breathing often changes. These changes in breathing can cause someone's asthma symptoms to get worse. This is an important trigger to talk to a doctor about because it's impossible to avoid having feelings!

important for people with asthma to stay away from people who are smoking.

In some cases, getting sick with the flu, a cold, or a sore throat can make asthma worse, especially for kids. Washing hands and staying away from people who are sick are ways to avoid this asthma trigger.

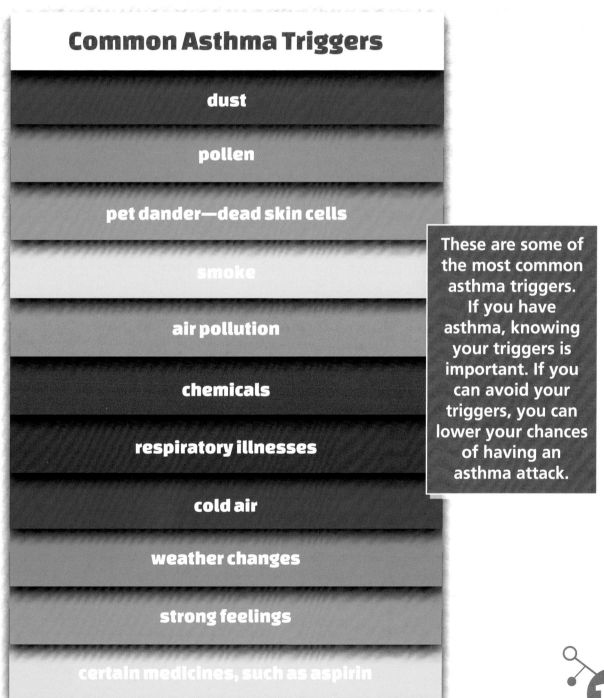

Common Asthma Triggers

dust

pollen

pet dander—dead skin cells

smoke

air pollution

chemicals

respiratory illnesses

cold air

weather changes

strong feelings

certain medicines, such as aspirin

These are some of the most common asthma triggers. If you have asthma, knowing your triggers is important. If you can avoid your triggers, you can lower your chances of having an asthma attack.

ALLERGIES AND ASTHMA

If breathing in pollen or pet dander causes someone's asthma to act up, they most likely have allergic asthma. This kind of asthma produces symptoms when someone breathes in an allergen, which is something they're allergic to. Pollen and pet dander are common allergens. Dust mites—tiny creatures that live in dust—and **mold** often trigger allergic asthma too.

A Special Doctor

If someone thinks they have asthma, especially allergic asthma, they often go to a doctor called an allergist, who deals with allergies. An allergist uses special tests to find out what someone is allergic to. One kind of test is a blood test. Another kind is a skin test. During a skin test, the allergist puts small amounts of allergens under someone's skin to see if they cause an allergic reaction, which often creates swelling and redness.

When someone has allergic asthma, their body thinks an allergen is harmful when it's not. When that allergen enters the body, the immune system—the part of the body that protects it from getting sick—tries to get rid of the allergen the same way it gets rid of germs. This generally includes inflammation and producing more mucus. This **reaction** causes many asthma symptoms.

Not everyone who has allergies also has asthma, and not everyone who has asthma has allergic asthma. However, allergic asthma is the most common kind of asthma.

STAYING ACTIVE WITH ASTHMA

For many years, people believed exercise could cause asthma. Today, doctors believe that's not true. However, exercise can make symptoms worse in people who do have asthma. This is because of a condition that's known as exercise-induced bronchoconstriction (EIB). This name comes from the fact that if someone has this problem, exercise constricts, or narrows, their bronchial tubes.

Asthma in the Spotlight

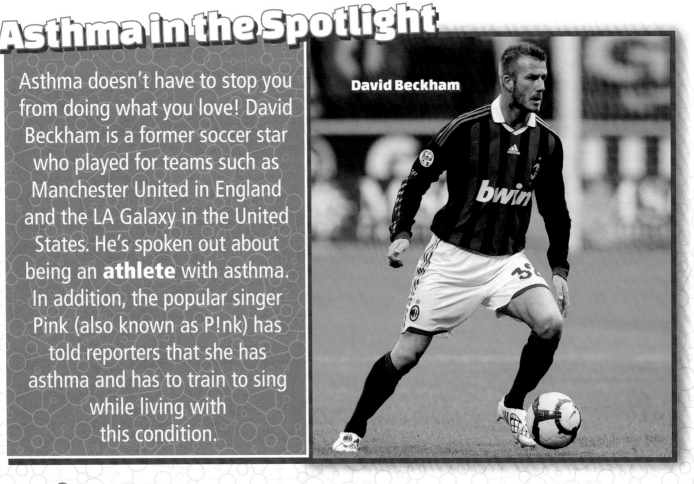

Asthma doesn't have to stop you from doing what you love! David Beckham is a former soccer star who played for teams such as Manchester United in England and the LA Galaxy in the United States. He's spoken out about being an **athlete** with asthma. In addition, the popular singer Pink (also known as P!nk) has told reporters that she has asthma and has to train to sing while living with this condition.

David Beckham

Although exercise doesn't cause asthma, 90 percent of people with asthma also have EIB, so EIB can play a part in making asthma symptoms, such as asthma attacks, worse. In some cases, exercising or playing sports outside can also expose people to allergic asthma triggers such as pollen.

People who have EIB can take medicine before they exercise to help control their asthma symptoms. They should also properly warm up before exercising.

Playing sports or doing other kinds of exercise is an important part of staying healthy, and it's fun! EIB doesn't have to stop anyone from being active as long as a helpful treatment plan is in place.

A VISIT TO THE ALLERGIST

Life can get better for people with asthma. The first step is seeing a doctor—most often an allergist. An allergist generally starts by asking their patient about their asthma symptoms, including what seems to cause them and how often they happen. They also ask questions about everyday life so they can find out if there's been any exposure to possible allergens.

Pass It On

Asthma often runs in families, which means if a parent has asthma, their children are more likely to have it too. Some doctors believe this is because some **genes** make people more likely to have allergies, which are a major cause of asthma. It's important to know your family history of health problems, including asthma. This makes it easier for doctors to know what conditions you might be at risk for having now and as you get older.

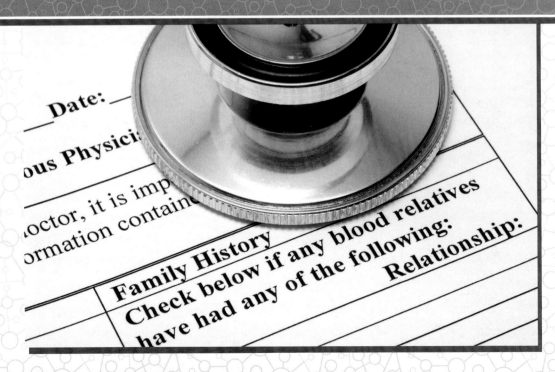

Then, the doctor often goes through certain tests that can help them make a diagnosis—a formal statement that someone has a medical problem such as asthma. One of these tests uses a tool called a spirometer. The patient takes a deep breath and then blows into a tube, which is connected to a device that measures how well they can breathe. Other tests sometimes include allergy tests and chest X-rays.

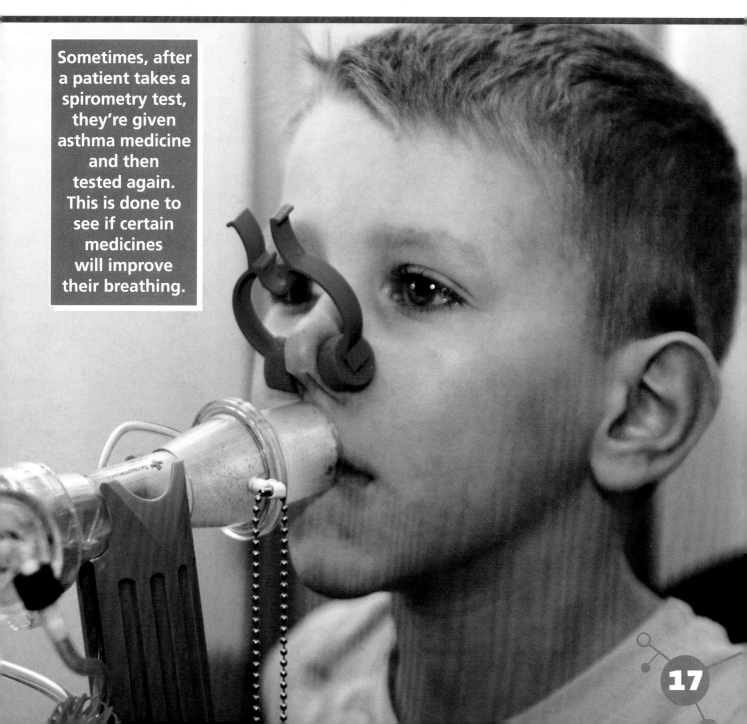

Sometimes, after a patient takes a spirometry test, they're given asthma medicine and then tested again. This is done to see if certain medicines will improve their breathing.

17

TAKING ACTION

If someone gets an official asthma diagnosis from a doctor, the next step is coming up with an asthma action plan to manage and treat the problem. This is a written plan that's often broken up into green, yellow, and red sections based on asthma symptoms and how long those symptoms have lasted.

Sharing the Plan

An asthma action plan is meant to be kept in a place at home that's easy to find and also shared with anyone who might need it. This includes anyone who watches a child with asthma, such as family members and babysitters. In addition, teachers, school nurses, and other school officials should always be given a copy of a child's asthma action plan. Because exercise often makes asthma symptoms worse, coaches should have their own copy too.

The green part of the plan states what kinds of medicines should be taken when asthma symptoms are under control. The yellow part breaks down what to do if asthma symptoms start getting worse, including what other medicines to take and when to call a doctor. In the red part of the asthma action plan, directions are given for an **emergency** situation. This includes when to call 911 and get the person to a hospital.

Many asthma action plans call for measurements from a peak flow meter. This is a tool that someone with asthma can carry with them to measure how well air is coming out of their lungs.

MEDICINE AND MANAGEMENT

Taking medicine is an important part of an asthma action plan, and there are two main kinds of medicine used to manage asthma symptoms. Long-term control medicines are generally taken every day, even when someone with asthma isn't experiencing symptoms. These medicines work over time to control mucus production and reduce airway inflammation. This can help control asthma and prevent uncomfortable symptoms.

Allergy Shots

Some people with allergic asthma feel better after getting allergy shots, which is a process known as immunotherapy. Allergy shots contain small amounts of an allergen, such as pollen. They're injected, or put, into a person's body for several years. Over that period of time, the immune system gets used to the allergen. When that happens, inflammation goes down, and allergy symptoms go away. Although allergy shots can help people with asthma, medicines are still the main way to treat this condition.

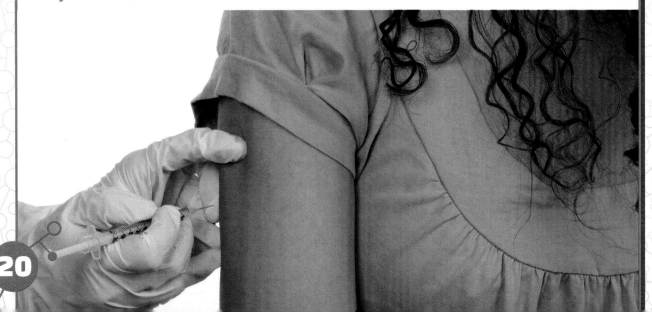

The other kind of asthma medicine is quick-relief medicine, which is sometimes called rescue medicine. Quick-relief medicine works fast to stop asthma symptoms, and it's often used during an asthma attack. It allows more air to flow through the bronchial tubes, and it helps clear mucus out of the airways. If you need quick-relief medicine for asthma, you should always keep it with you.

It's important for someone with asthma to monitor, or closely watch, their symptoms to make sure their medicine doesn't need to change. For example, if a person needs to use their quick-relief medicine more than twice each week, they should talk to their doctor about trying a different medicine to better manage their symptoms.

THE INS AND OUTS OF INHALERS

Some asthma medicines are taken as pills or liquids, but many are inhaled, or breathed in. This kind of medicine is taken using an inhaler, which is supposed to send the medicine to the airways that need it.

A Doctor's Directions

If you need to use an inhaler, make sure you carefully follow your doctor's directions. For example, a metered-dose inhaler needs to be shaken before it's used, but a dry powder inhaler generally doesn't need to be shaken. It's important to feel comfortable using your inhaler, so don't be afraid to ask questions about how to use it properly. Also, make sure you know how many puffs of medicine from your inhaler you're supposed to take.

dry powder inhaler

A metered-dose inhaler **releases** a puff of medicine when someone pushes down on the top of it. A person should breathe in as the medicine is being released so it can get to work opening the airways. In many cases, people use a spacer, which is also called a holding chamber, to make sure the medicine goes directly to the airways instead of the mouth or throat.

A dry powder inhaler releases medicine when a person breathes into it. You don't need to press its top down like a metered-dose inhaler.

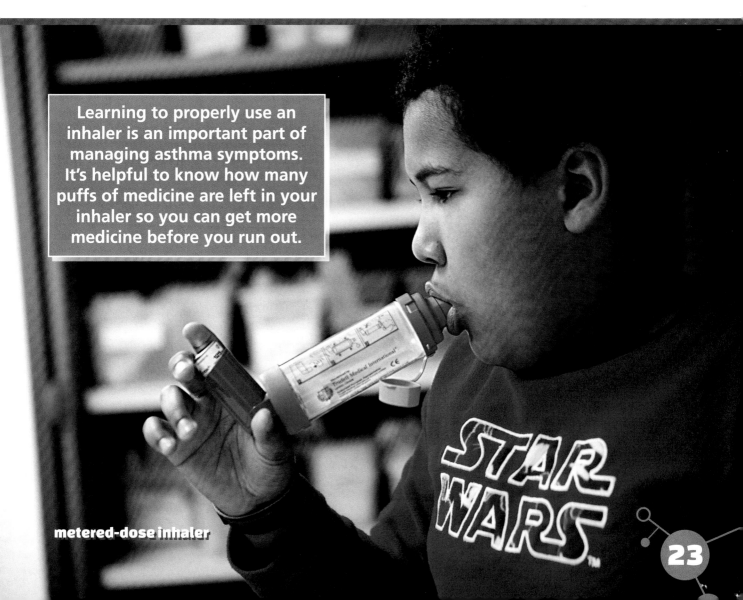

Learning to properly use an inhaler is an important part of managing asthma symptoms. It's helpful to know how many puffs of medicine are left in your inhaler so you can get more medicine before you run out.

metered-dose inhaler

NEEDING A NEBULIZER

In some cases, a person with asthma might not use an inhaler. Instead, they might use a nebulizer. This is a machine that comes with a mouthpiece or mask that a person wears over their nose and mouth. The machine turns liquid asthma medicine into a mist. Then, the person with asthma breathes in the mist through the mouthpiece or mask.

Nebulizers take longer than inhalers to get medicine into the airways. It often takes at least 10 minutes for all the medicine to get into the body. A person can read a book or watch TV while using their nebulizer. Nebulizers are also bigger to carry around than inhalers. However, many young children use nebulizers because inhalers are too hard for them to use.

Keep It Clean!

It's important to keep nebulizers and inhalers clean. This keeps them working properly and keeps the people who use them from getting sick. Each device is different, so the directions for that specific device must be followed closely. However, many parts of these devices, including the mouthpiece or mask of a nebulizer, can be cleaned with water or a cloth. It's also good to clean your mouth with water or mouthwash after using an inhaler.

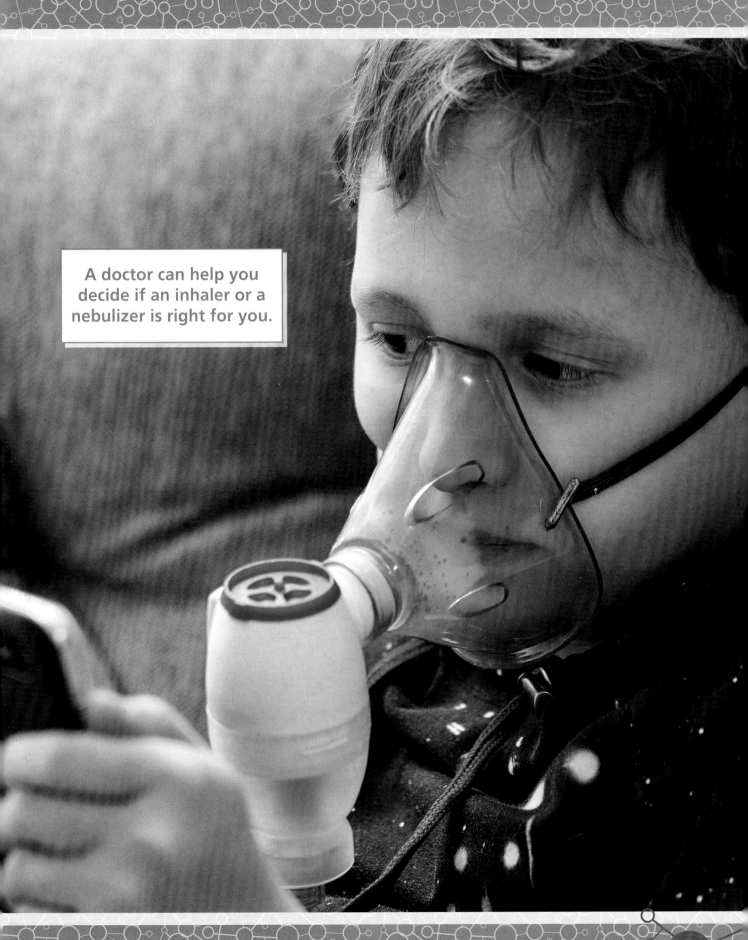

A doctor can help you decide if an inhaler or a nebulizer is right for you.

BE PREPARED!

If you have asthma, it's important to be prepared. Know your action plan, and carry a copy of it with you. Follow your doctor's directions for taking your medicine, and take your quick-relief medicine with you to school, to practices and games for sports, and even on vacation.

It can be hard talking about health problems, but it's helpful to tell your teachers, coaches, and close friends you have asthma. They need to know so they can help you quickly if you have an asthma attack.

Even if you don't have asthma, it's important to be prepared to help someone else who might have it. If you have a friend or family member who's living with asthma, ask them about their action plan and what you can do to help.

You're Not Alone

If you have asthma, it's helpful to know you're not alone. Some communities have special groups that meet—called support groups—to help each other deal with problems, such as asthma. People in a support group are generally all dealing with the same problem, so they can help each other feel understood. Some support groups are for people who are living with health problems, and others are for parents or children of these people.

How can you help someone with asthma?

! Help them avoid asthma triggers. For example, if cold air triggers their asthma symptoms, invite them to play inside during the winter.

! Ask them if they want to share their action plan. If they choose to share it with you, read it, and learn how you can help in an emergency.

! If they're having an asthma attack, stay calm, and try to find an adult to help. If there's no adult around, help them use their inhaler.

! If exercise makes their asthma worse, warm up with them before playing a sport.

! Treat them with respect, and never tease them about their asthma.

! Remind them that asthma doesn't have to stop them from having fun.

It can be hard to deal with asthma, but these are some ways you can help make it easier for a friend or family member living with this condition.

ASTHMA ON THE RISE

Asthma is on the rise in the United States, so doctors are working hard to learn more about this health problem. They're studying things that make someone more likely to have asthma, including obesity—the state of being very overweight. They're also learning more about how air pollution affects asthma. In fact, there are now air quality warnings to help people with asthma know that the level of air pollution might make it hard for them to breathe.

Asthma might seem scary, but it's important to remember that it's a health problem that can be controlled. With careful monitoring, medicine, and a strong understanding of this condition and its triggers, people with asthma can be just as active, healthy, and happy as everyone else!

Can You Outgrow It?

Some people who had asthma as children don't seem to have it anymore as adults. This has led many people to believe that you can outgrow asthma. However, doctors often state that asthma never fully goes away. While the symptoms may seem to stop, there's still a chance they could come back. In other cases, people who seem to have outgrown asthma may have been **misdiagnosed** with it in the first place.

If you have asthma, it doesn't have to control your life. Instead, you can come up with a plan to control your asthma so the only thing you need to think about is having fun.

Glossary

athlete: A person who plays a sport.

emergency: An unexpected and often unsafe situation that calls for immediate action.

fluid: A substance that flows freely like water.

gene: One of the parts of cells considered the building blocks of a living thing that control the appearance, growth, and other qualities of a living thing.

misdiagnose: To incorrectly say that someone has a health problem they don't actually have.

mold: A fuzzy growth of fungus that often forms on damp material.

reaction: The act of doing something because of something else that has happened.

release: To allow to escape or get out.

treatment: Care given to a person or animal that is sick.

For More Information

WEBSITES

CDC: Asthma—Kids

www.cdc.gov/asthma/children.htm

Visitors to this website can listen to podcasts, watch videos, and check out links to other websites that are helpful for kids living with asthma.

KidsHealth: Asthma Center

kidshealth.org/en/kids/center/asthma-center.html

The KidsHealth Asthma Center has all the facts you need to be as educated as possible about asthma.

BOOKS

Duhig, Holly. *Understanding Asthma*. King's Lynn, England: BookLife Publishing, 2018.

Levine, Michelle. *Asthma*. Mankato, MN: Amicus Publishing, 2015.

Nunn, Laura Silverstein, Virginia Silverstein, and Alvin Silverstein. *Handy Health Guide to Asthma*. Berkeley Heights, NJ: Enslow Publishing, 2014.

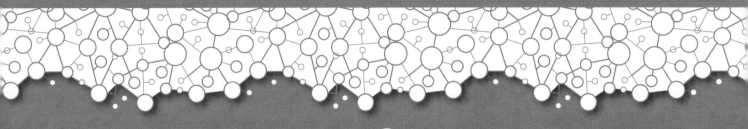

Index